T0268506

SPACESHIPS
AND
ROCKETS

FIRST EDITION
Series Editor Deborah Lock; **US Senior Editor** Shannon Beatty; **Art Director** Martin Wilson;
Picture Researcher Surya Sarangi; **Producer, Pre-Production** Nadine King;
Reading Consultant Linda Gambrell, PhD

THIS EDITION
Editorial Management by Oriel Square
Produced for DK by WonderLab Group LLC
Jennifer Emmett, Erica Green, Kate Hale, *Founders*

Editors Grace Hill Smith, Libby Romero, Maya Myers, Michaela Weglinski;
Photography Editors Kelley Miller, Annette Kiesow, Nicole DiMella; **Managing Editor** Rachel Houghton;
Designers Project Design Company; **Researcher** Michelle Harris; **Copy Editor** Lori Merritt;
Indexer Connie Binder; **Proofreader** Larry Shea; **Reading Specialist** Dr. Jennifer Albro;
Curriculum Specialist Elaine Larson

Published in the United States by DK Publishing
1745 Broadway, 20th Floor, New York, NY 10019
Copyright © 2023 Dorling Kindersley Limited
DK, a Division of Penguin Random House LLC
23 24 25 26 10 9 8 7 6 5 4 3 2
003-334117-Sept/2023

A catalog record for this book
is available from the Library of Congress.
HC ISBN: 978-0-7440-7541-0
PB ISBN: 978-0-7440-7543-4

DK books are available at special discounts when purchased in bulk for sales promotions, premiums,
fundraising, or educational use. For details, contact: DK Publishing Special Markets,
1745 Broadway, 20th Floor, New York, NY 10019
SpecialSales@dk.com

Printed and bound in China

The publisher would like to thank the following for their kind permission to reproduce their images:
a=above; c=center; b=below; l=left; r=right; t=top; b/g=background
Alamy Stock Photo: Blue Origin 26br; **Dreamstime.com:** Nexusplexus 30b; **Fotolia:** Stephen Sweet 3cb;
NASA: MSFC / Brandon Hancock 1, 10; **Shutterstock.com:** Oleg_Yakovlev 4-5
Cover images: *Front:* **Shutterstock.com:** Evgeniyqw; *Back:* **Shutterstock.com:** TyBy cla

All other images © Dorling Kindersley
For more information see: www.dkimages.com

For the curious
www.dk.com

SPACESHIPS
AND
ROCKETS

Deborah Lock

Contents

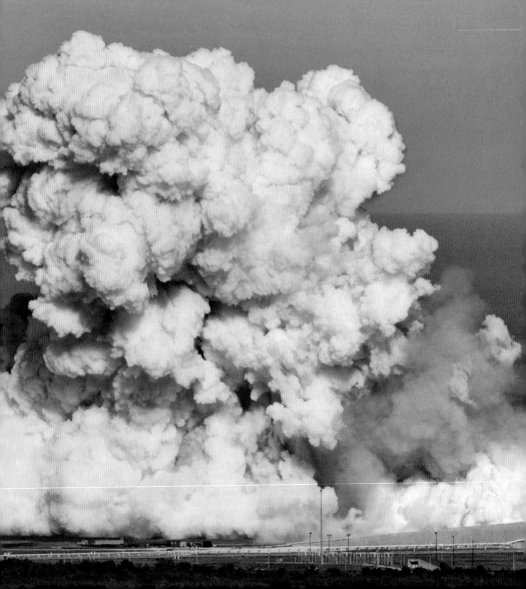

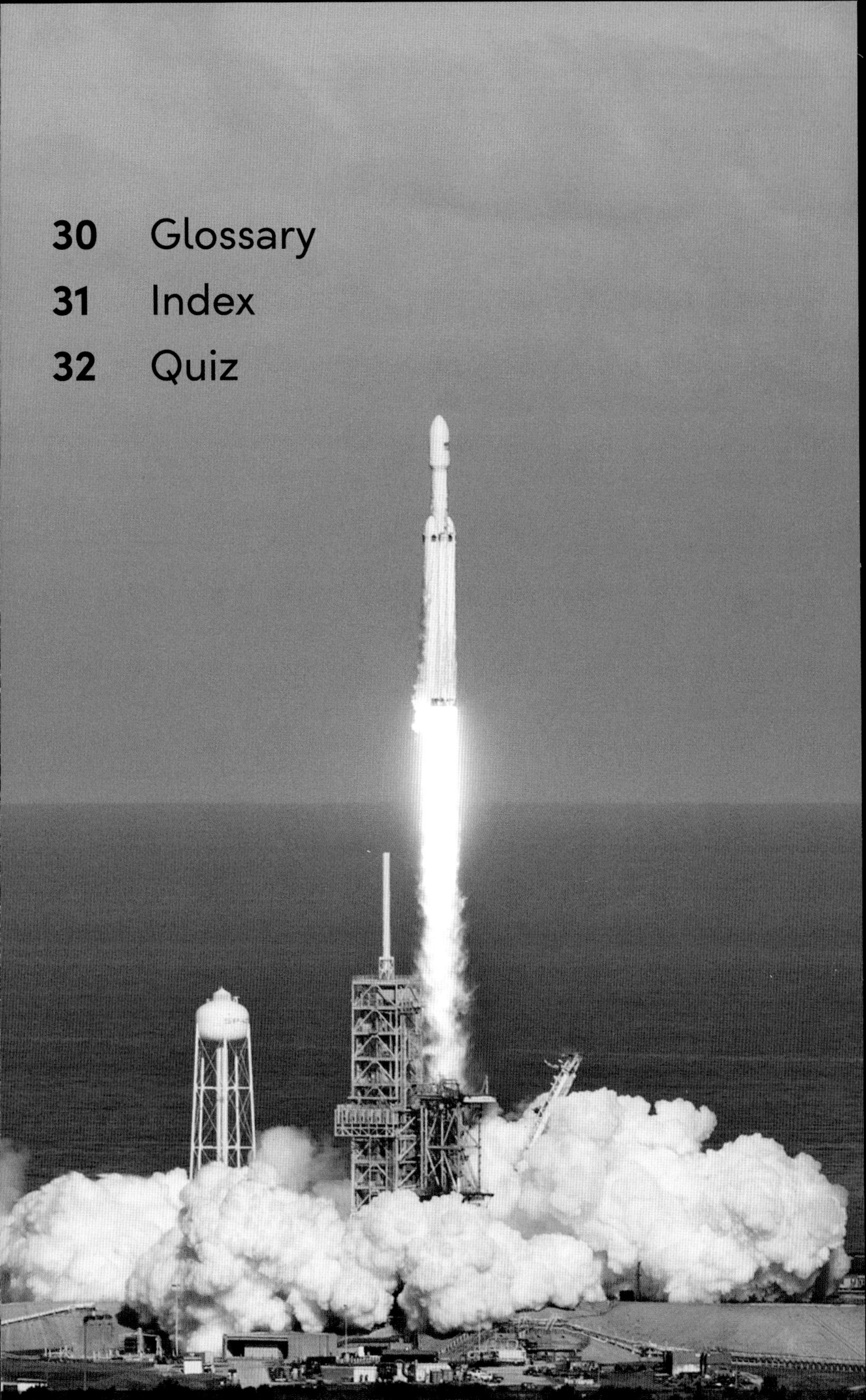

The Launch

5 The rocket points to the sky. It is ready to launch.

4 The engines spark. Flames and smoke billow out.

3 The rocket shakes and rumbles.

2 The engines roar.

1 Blast off!

Parts of a Rocket

Rockets are made up of many parts or stages. The booster rockets give extra power for launch.

Size Guide
(rocket versus African elephant)

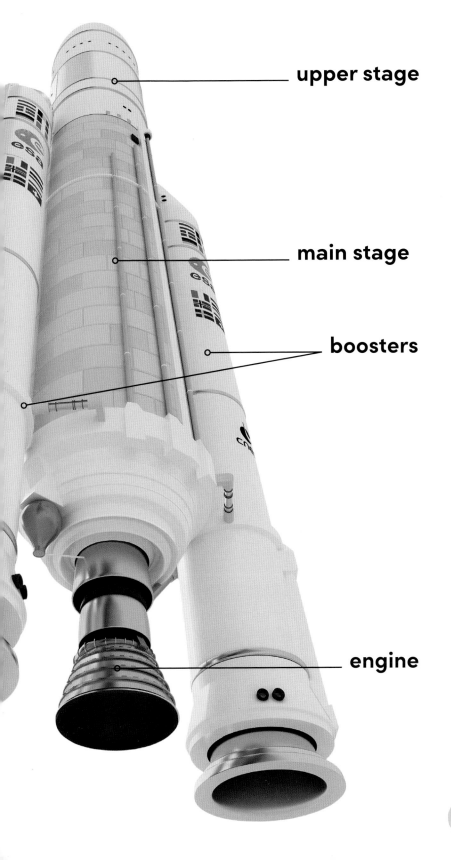

upper stage

main stage

boosters

engine

Up, up! The rocket zooms into the sky.

The engines power the rocket higher and higher. The rocket now looks like a tiny speck in the sky. The boosters drop away.

The rocket fires its smaller engine. It zooms upward, faster and faster.

It passes through the thin layer of gases around Earth. The rocket breaks through into the darkness of space.

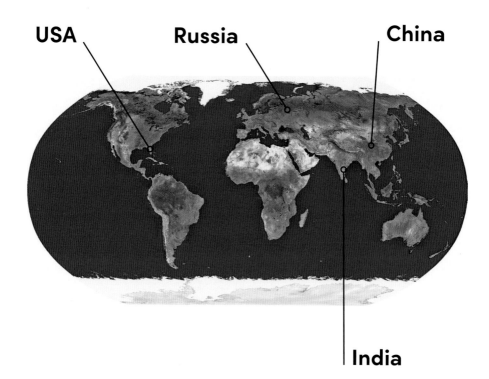

USA   **Russia**   **China**

India

Launch Sites

Countries around
the world have
launched rockets.
Here are some of
the launch sites.

Each rocket that blasts off has a job to do—a mission.

These missions can last a few days or a few weeks. Some missions can last for years and years.

Crewed Missions

Some rockets carry people into space. This rocket is called Vostok 1 [VOH-stock].

It took the first person to space in 1961. His name was Yuri Gagarin [YOUR-ee ga-GAR-een]. He was Russian.

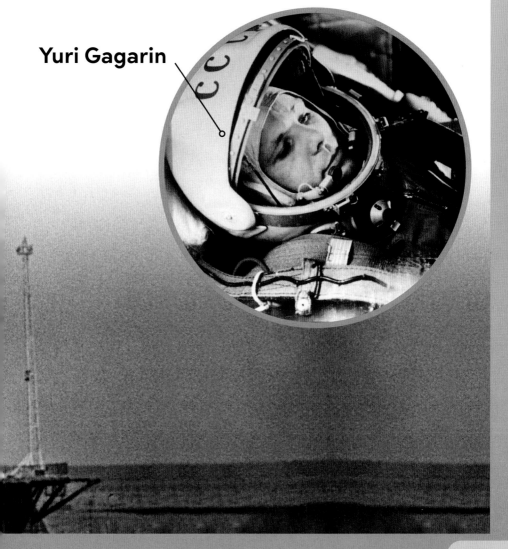

Yuri Gagarin

In July, 1969, the Saturn V (5) rocket took Apollo 11 astronauts to the Moon. At the time, it was the largest rocket ever built. The astronauts sat in a small capsule on top of the rocket.

Apollo 11

The Apollo 11 capsule contained two parts. The Command and Service Module, called *Columbia*, stayed in space. The Lunar Module, called *Eagle*, took astronauts to the Moon's surface.

This is a space shuttle. Space shuttles took off on a rocket and landed as a plane. They were used to take astronauts into space many times.

These astronauts visited
a space station and did
space walks.

Some rockets now take tourists for a trip into space. This is the Russian rocket Soyuz [SU-yoos].

At the top of the rocket is a spacecraft that takes people to the International Space Station. They stay for a week.

Expensive Vacation

A one-week trip to the International Space Station costs around $50 million. While there, tourists work in the lab, exercise to keep fit, eat space food, and strap in to sleep—just like the professional astronauts do.

Uncrewed Missions

Some rockets carry satellites and probes into space. Satellites are machines. They travel around, or orbit, Earth. Satellites send back pictures and messages to Earth.

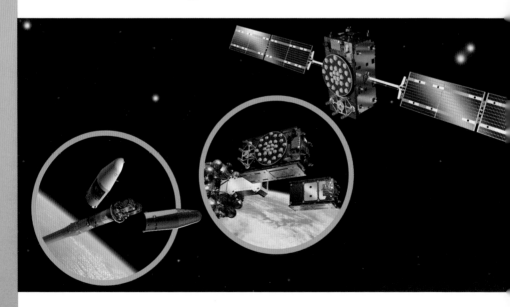

The Ariane 5 [ah-ree-AH-ne] rocket can carry two heavy satellites.

The Rosetta [roh–SET-tah] probe flew past asteroids.

Probes are small, unmanned spacecraft. Probes fly to planets and explore space. They send back pictures and other data to Earth.

In 1977, a Titan–Centaur [TI-tan-SEN-tor] rocket carried Voyager 1 and 2 into space. The Voyager probes have been flying for more than 40 years.

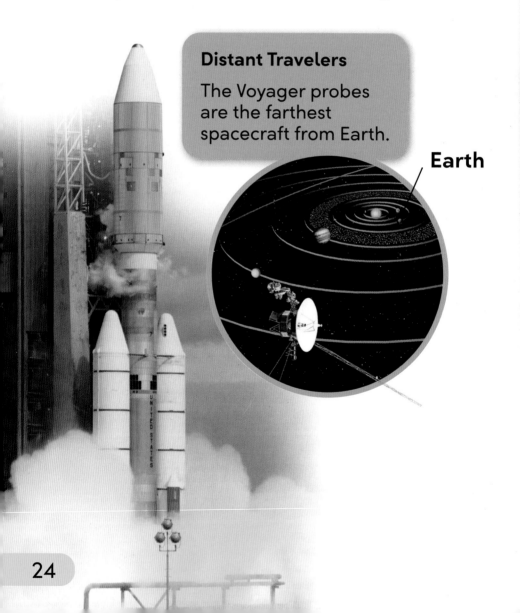

Distant Travelers

The Voyager probes are the farthest spacecraft from Earth.

Earth

The Pathfinder probe landed on Mars in 1997. It needed a very large parachute to slow down. It landed a small, robotic vehicle called a rover.

Sojourner

The Sojourner rover was the first robot to do tests on Mars.

Future Missions

Would you like to go on a trip into space? Spacecraft are now taking passengers on trips into sub-orbit. The passengers feel like they are floating for a few minutes. Then, the spacecraft returns to Earth.

There are many ideas for a future in space. Spaceplanes could take off from runways. Spacecraft could take passengers on trips to space hotels.

Spacecraft could take astronauts to Mars and beyond, too.

Think about the future. Once we reach Mars, will we build stations and live there? How much farther into space can we go? Would you like to be a space traveler someday?

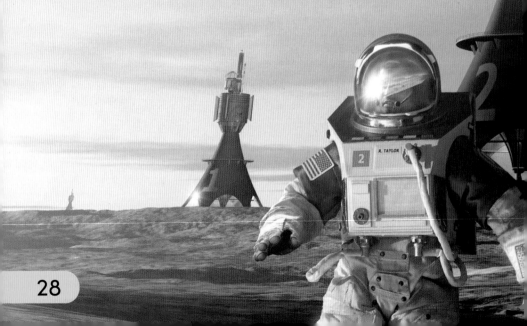

Glossary

Astronaut
A person who has been trained to travel inside a spacecraft

Booster
A part of a rocket that gives extra speed and power at liftoff

Capsule
A part of a spacecraft that people travel in and that often splits away from the rocket

Lab (Laboratory)
A place where science tests are carried out

Orbit
The path an object makes around another object

Passenger
A person who travels, but is not the driver

Probe
An uncrewed spacecraft that sends information about space back to Earth

Rover
A robotic vehicle that explores the surface of planets

Satellite
An object that orbits another

Spacecraft
A vehicle or probe designed to travel in space

Space station
A space lab that orbits Earth with astronauts living there

Index

Quiz

Answer the questions to see what you have learned. Check your answers in the key below.

1. In what year did the first person go into space?

2. What kind of rocket took Apollo 11 astronauts to the Moon?

3. Which probes have traveled the farthest from Earth?

4. How many satellites can Ariane 5 carry?

5. Where did the Pathfinder probe land?

1. 1961 2. Saturn V 3. Voyager 1 and Voyager 2 4. Two 5. Mars